I0436586

# Innovate to Elevate: Business Strategies for the Modern Entrepreneur

Jane J. Whitney

# TABLE OF CONTENT

# Chapter 1

## The Power of Innovation in Business

Innovation promotes constant improvement, environment adaption, and market distinction, innovation gives businesses a significant competitive edge. An examination of the ways in which innovation gives a competitive edge is provided below:

✓ Market Differentiation:- Unique goods, services, or methods help a business stand out from rivals.
    - Distinctiveness draws clients and can position a company as a leader in its field.

✓ Meeting Customer Needs: - Businesses can better understand and meet customer needs when they use innovation.

- Improving customer satisfaction requires adapting to changing preferences and expectations.

✓ Increased Efficiency:- Cutting-edge procedures and technological advancements increase productivity.
   - A competitive cost advantage is a result of lower expenses and increased productivity.

✓ Adaptability to Change:- Innovative companies can react swiftly to changes in the market, in regulations, or in technology. - They are more adaptive to changes in the business environment.

✓ Enhanced Problem-Solving:- A creative problem-solving mindset is fostered by an innovative culture.
   - Organizations can gain a competitive advantage by skillfully overcoming obstacles.

✓ Attracting and Retaining Talent:- Forward-thinking businesses draw top talent looking for stimulating and creative work environments.

- A reputation for innovation aids in luring in talented workers dedicated to ongoing development.

✓ Decision-Making Agility:

- A culture of experimentation and learning from mistakes is fostered by innovation.

- Businesses grow more adept at making decisions and react quickly to possibilities in the market.

✓ Market Leadership: - A business that maintains a constant state of innovation is positioned to lead its industry.

- Greater market share and influence might result from becoming a market leader.

✓ Strategic Partnerships: - Other industry participants frequently look to innovative enterprises as strategic partners.

- Partnerships increase capacities and create new growth opportunities.

✓ Loyalty to Customers:
  - Relentless innovation keeps clients interested and faithful.
  - Long-term client relationships can result from consistently presenting new and improved goods.

✓ Risk Management:- Businesses can diversify and investigate new revenue streams with the aid of innovation.
  - The hazards connected with depending too much on one good or service might be reduced by having a diversified portfolio.

✓ Global Competitiveness:- Innovative methods improve a business's ability to compete internationally.
  - Being able to innovate in business concepts or technology can lead to success abroad.

✓ Long-Term Sustainability: - Long-term relevance is ensured by innovating with sustainability in mind.

- Resolving social and environmental issues can enhance favorable brand perception.

✓ Brand Resilience: - Customers and stakeholders are more confident when a brand is known for its innovation.
- Brands that are resilient are better able to weather difficulties and emergencies.

To put it simply, using innovation as a competitive advantage means being ahead of the curve, seeing changes coming, and continuously providing value in ways that are difficult for competitors to match. It is a dynamic force that helps businesses succeed over the long term in a business environment that is changing quickly.

**The following are examples of inventive, successful businesses:**

Apple Inc.: - With devices like the iPhone, iPad, and MacBook, Apple transformed the tech sector.

- Continuous innovation in user experience, functionality, and design.

Tesla: - With its electric cars and environmentally friendly energy solutions, Tesla upended the auto sector.
   - Constant innovation in autonomous driving and battery technologies.

Google: - Google revolutionized online advertising and search.
   - Digital innovations such as Android, Gmail, and Google Maps have influenced the environment.

Amazon: - Amazon revolutionized the retail industry with its e-commerce and logistics innovations.
   - Kindle e-readers, AWS, and Prime shipping are examples of innovations.

Netflix: - The company's streaming services upended the entertainment sector. - Its original content creation and tailored suggestions are its two main advances.

Airbnb: - With its peer-to-peer lodging network, Airbnb revolutionized the hospitality sector.
 - Innovation in community development and user experience.

SpaceX: - Using reusable rocket technology, SpaceX transformed space exploration.
 - Innovation in bringing down the price of space travel and increasing accessibility.

Alibaba Group: - Alibaba transformed digital payments and e-commerce in China.
 - Taobao, Alipay, and the diversification into other industries are examples of innovations.

Facebook: - The social networking giant's innovations changed the way people communicate online. - Its impact was furthered by acquisitions such as Instagram and WhatsApp.

IBM: - From mainframes to cloud computing and artificial intelligence, IBM has continuously reinvented itself.

- Advancements in data analytics, quantum computing, and corporate solutions.

Zoom: Zoom revolutionized online communication and video conferencing.

- During the COVID-19 epidemic, rapid innovation resulted in broad acceptance.

These case studies demonstrate the various ways that innovation has fueled success in a variety of sectors, emphasizing the need of staying ahead of the curve and adjusting to shifting conditions.

Encouraging creativity, teamwork, and a willingness to take chances are all part of cultivating an innovative culture inside a business.

**The following are some tactics to foster a creative culture:**

Leadership Support:- Innovation projects should be aggressively promoted and supported by leadership.

- Establish the tone by encouraging an attitude that welcomes experimentation and change.

Unambiguous Vision and Objectives:

-Clearly convey the company's mission and objectives for innovation.

- Align innovation initiatives with overarching corporate goals.

Promote Open Communication:- Establish lines of communication that are open to all parties.

Encourage staff members to openly express their thoughts, opinions, and concerns.

Set Apart Time for Originality:

- Give staff members specific time for introspection and creativity.

- Introduce "innovation time" or project-specific initiatives that promote experimentation.

Interaction with Cross-Functions:

- Encourage cooperation amongst various teams and departments.
- Promote a diversity of viewpoints and expertise to spark original thought.

Reward and Recognition: - Give credit for creative endeavors and well-thought-out concepts.

Recognize contributions of all sizes to promote an attitude of gratitude.

Learning and Development Opportunities:- Make training program investments to advance staff members' expertise.

- Offer chances for lifelong learning and career advancement.

Mistakes as Teaching Tools:

- Promote an attitude that sees setbacks as chances to grow.
- Examine setbacks, draw conclusions, and use those insights in subsequent attempts.

Challenges and Competitions for Innovation:
- Arrange contests or challenges that foster inventiveness.
- Offer rewards to staff members who engage and present their creative ideas.

Spaces or Labs for Innovation:
- Establish locations, either real or virtual, where staff members may think and work together.
- Establish an atmosphere that encourages independent thought and innovation.

Consumer-Centric Approach: - Promote a thorough comprehension of the requirements and preferences of the consumer.
- Encourage staff members to approach problem-solving from the viewpoint of the client.

Embrace Technology: - Make cutting-edge instruments and technology available.
- Use technology to advance research, development, and teamwork.

Inclusive Decision-Making: - Involve staff members at all levels in decision-making procedures.

Make sure a variety of opinions are heard while determining the company's course.

Strategic Partnerships: - Establish alliances with outside groups to introduce new viewpoints.

- Work together with startups, academic institutions, or business specialists.

Constantial Innovation Evaluations:

- Regularly evaluate the business's innovative initiatives.

- Modify plans in response to comments and changing business requirements.

Social Responsibility and Sustainability:- Promote innovation in line with social responsibility and sustainability.

- Find innovative answers to society problems. Through the application of these tactics, an organization may establish a flexible and dynamic culture that recognizes innovation as a fundamental component of its character. As a result, the company is better positioned for long-term profitability and resilience in a business climate that is changing quickly.

# Chapter 2

## Digital Transformation: Navigating the Tech Revolution

In today's quickly changing corporate environment, adopting digital trends and technologies is crucial to maintaining competitiveness and promoting business expansion. The following tactics will help you successfully integrate digital trends into your company:

**Continuous Learning**: - Encourage a culture of ongoing education to keep staff members abreast of technological advancements.
   - Promote involvement in industry events and training programs.

**Digital Transformation Strategy**:- Create a well-defined plan for digital transformation that is in line with corporate objectives.

   - Set priorities in areas where digitization can have the most influence.

**Data-Driven Decision-Making**:- Stress the significance of making decisions based on data.

   - Make an investment in analytics procedures and tools to use data to get insights.

**Cloud Computing**:- Adopt cloud computing to take advantage of its scalability, flexibility, and affordability.

   - Convert pertinent processes and services to cloud computing platforms.

**Mobile Optimization**:- Make sure mobile consumers' digital experiences are optimized.

   Make sure apps and webpages are adaptable to different screen sizes and easy to use.

**AI and Machine Learning**: - Examine how AI and machine learning may be used for predictive analytics and automation.

   - Use virtual assistants or chatbots to improve customer service.

**Cybersecurity Measures**:- Give cybersecurity first priority in order to safeguard consumer information and digital assets.

   - Remain up to date on the newest risks to cybersecurity and recommended procedures.

**E-Commerce Integration**:- Expand online sales channels by integrating e-commerce systems, if available.

   - Improve the general client experience by implementing smooth online transactions.

**Digital Marketing Strategies**: - To reach a larger audience, make an investment in digital marketing.

   - To improve online presence, use SEO, social media, and content marketing.

**Collaboration Tools**: - Put collaboration tools into practice to make remote work easier and communication more efficient.

- Use project management tools to facilitate productive collaboration.

**Technology Of Blockchain**:
Examine how blockchain technology may be used to facilitate safe and open transactions.

Analyze how blockchain technology may improve operations and your industry.

**Internet of Things (IoT):**- Implement IoT devices to gather data and optimize processes.

Investigate Internet of Things applications that improve consumer experiences or product functioning.

**Improving the Customer Experience**: - Use digital technology to improve the clientele's experience in general.

- Use feedback channels and customization to adjust services.

**Agile Development Practices:-** Use agile development techniques to create software more quickly and adaptably.

- Adopt iterative strategies to react fast to evolving needs.

**Infrastructure for Remote Work**:- Make an investment in the technological infrastructure necessary to enable remote work.

- Assure staff members have the resources they need for productive online teamwork.

**Subscription-Based Models**:- If you want to generate recurring income, think about using subscription-based business models.

Make use of digital channels to provide subscription services.

**Visual and Audio Search:**

- As voice and visual search become more common, optimize for them.
- Remain aware of modifications to user behavior and search engine algorithms.

Businesses may position themselves for development and innovation in the digital era and adapt to the changing landscape by adopting these digital trends and technology. To keep ahead of the curve, evaluate industry trends on a regular basis and execute digital plans quickly.

Putting into practice digital transformation plans that work is essential for companies looking to improve productivity, performance, and competitiveness. The following is a manual for carrying out a successful digital transformation:

✓ Leadership Commitment:- Get the support and motivation for digital transformation from the top leadership.
  - The organization as a whole should be informed by leadership on the goals and advantages of digitization.

✓ Establish Clearly Defined Objectives: - Clearly state the aims and purposes of the digital transformation process.

- For a cogent approach, match these objectives with the overarching company plan.

✓ Interaction of Cross-Functions:
- Encourage cooperation amongst various teams and departments.
- Assure that different stakeholders participate in and gain from the activities pertaining to digital transformation.

✓ Customer-Centric Approach:- Give projects that improve the customer experience top priority.
Recognize the requirements and expectations of your customers to direct your digital transformation initiatives.

✓ Evaluate Present Situation:
- Evaluate the organization's present digital capabilities in-depth.
Determine your advantages, disadvantages, and places in need of development.

✓ Technology Infrastructure: - Make a significant investment to support digital activities with a strong technology infrastructure.
  - Make sure it is flexible and scalable enough to adjust to changing technological trends.

✓ Data Governance and Analytics:- Create robust data governance procedures to guarantee the security and quality of your data.
  - Use analytics to obtain practical insights that guide choices.

✓ Agile Methodology:- Implement agile development and project management techniques.
  - Adopt iterative procedures to react fast to evolving needs.

✓ Upskilling and Employee Training:
  - Offer training courses to give staff members the essential digital abilities.
  - Promote an environment that values adaptation and ongoing learning.

✓ Change Management:- Create a strong change management plan to deal with opposition.

- Effectively communicate changes and include staff members in the transformation process.

✓ Security Measures:- Give cybersecurity first priority in order to safeguard sensitive data and digital assets.

- Put security measures into place that comply with industry norms.

✓ Pilot Programs: - Before implementing digital solutions widely, start with pilot programs to test and improve them.

- Use the lessons learned from pilot projects to enhance future ones.

✓ Vendor Partnerships: - Work together with partners and technology suppliers to take use of outside knowledge.

- Look into strategic alliances for creative fixes.

✓ Cloud Adoption:- Use cloud computing to boost cost-effectiveness, scalability, and agility.
   - Convert pertinent systems and programs to cloud computing environments.

✓ Measure and Iterate: - To gauge the effectiveness of digital projects, set up key performance indicators (KPIs).
   - Evaluate and refine tactics on a regular basis using performance indicators.

✓ Culture of Innovation: - Promote an innovative environment that rewards trial and error as well as taking calculated risks.
   Acknowledge and honor creative contributions made by the organization's members.

✓ Regulatory Compliance: - Keep up with and abide by industry rules pertaining to digital transformation.
   - Verify that digital efforts follow all applicable laws and regulations.

✓ Strategic Communication:- Share accomplishments and progress with the whole organization.

Make sure staff members are aware of the advantages and effects of the digital transition.

Organizations may successfully handle the challenges of digital transformation and make sure the process is impactful, well-managed, and in line with the overall company plan by using these techniques methodically.

In the ever-changing business landscape of today, companies are always looking for new and creative ways to get a competitive advantage and promote long-term success. Data analytics and artificial intelligence (AI) are two disruptive technologies that have become potent instruments capable of restructuring corporate processes, providing strategic guidance, and opening up previously unheard-of development prospects.

Unlocking meaningful insights from the abundance of information accessible to organizations is made possible in large part by data analytics, the process of analyzing and interpreting massive databases. Organizations may discover patterns, make well-informed selections, and comprehend client behavior better by utilizing data. Because of their ability to analyze data, firms are able to better satisfy and retain customers by customizing their offerings to match changing market demands. Additionally, data analytics helps businesses find opportunities for cost reductions, improve operations, and enhance internal procedures. By using predictive analytics, businesses may foresee customer preferences and market trends and strategically position themselves to react quickly to shifts in the industry. To put it simply, data analytics serves as a compass, pointing organizations in the direction of well-informed, data-driven decisions.

Artificial intelligence adds a new facet to corporate success by enhancing data analytics. Artificial intelligence (AI) technologies, such natural language processing and machine learning, enable businesses to automate tasks, obtain predictive insights, and increase productivity. For instance, machine learning algorithms may use past data to forecast future trends, giving businesses the ability to remain ahead of the curve in the market and make growth-oriented strategic decisions.

Personalized client experiences are a noteworthy use of AI in company expansion. Businesses may provide individualized services, recommendations, and communications based on the interests of each individual consumer by utilizing AI-driven customization. Long-term company growth is facilitated by this, which also raises brand loyalty and improves consumer happiness.

AI also makes it easier to create intelligent systems that can improve resource allocation, inventory control, and supply chain management. These clever solutions maximize efficiency while reducing waste as they adjust to changing conditions. In addition to saving money, this puts companies in a position to smoothly expand their operations in response to variations in demand.

AI and data analytics together have a significant influence on marketing strategy. Businesses may develop individualized and targeted marketing efforts by utilizing data-driven insights. By analyzing consumer behavior, forecasting trends, and streamlining marketing campaigns, artificial intelligence (AI) algorithms help companies make sure the appropriate message reaches the right audience at the right moment. This improves the overall efficacy of client acquisition and retention efforts in addition to optimizing marketing return on investment. While there is no denying that data analytics and artificial intelligence (AI) may help businesses thrive, companies also need to be aware of data protection, ethics, and appropriate usage of these tools. Establishing trust with stakeholders and consumers is critical to sustaining success, and companies need to give ethical and transparent data and AI processes a priority.

Organizations now have access to never-before-seen possibilities for development and competitiveness thanks to the synergistic combination of artificial intelligence and data analytics. These technologies enable businesses to tailor consumer experiences, optimize processes, and make data-driven choices. Businesses that effectively use AI and data analytics will not only survive the digital age, but prosper in a setting where creativity and flexibility are critical factors in long-term prosperity.

# Chapter 3

## Customer-Centric Approach: Building Strong Relationships

Successful and long-lasting business development starts with recognizing and satisfying client demands. It is more than just providing a good or service; it also entails building strong relationships with clients and meeting their expectations for value. This customer-focused strategy is extremely important for a number of reasons.

Businesses may obtain significant insights into the preferences, habits, and pain points of their target audience by understanding consumer demands. This knowledge serves as the cornerstone for developing goods and services that really meet the needs and overcome the obstacles of customers. Meeting client demands essentially guarantees that companies offer solutions that appeal to their target market, which promotes client happiness and loyalty.

Long-term success is largely dependent on customer loyalty. Businesses that continuously satisfy their consumers' requirements gain their trust and loyalty, which motivates them to make more purchases from them in the future. Customers that are happy with a brand have a higher probability of becoming brand ambassadors, generating favorable word-of-mouth referrals and assisting in the company's natural expansion.

Moreover, recognizing and satisfying client wants is a critical difference at a time of plenty of options and intense competition. Prioritizing client happiness helps businesses stand out from the competition and gain a competitive edge that extends beyond product features and cost. This distinction is especially important in markets where rivals may provide comparable goods or services.

Fulfilling client demands is a continuous process rather than a one-time event. Both markets and consumer expectations are dynamic. Companies who remain aware of these changes and modify their products and services appropriately set themselves up for long-term success. An adaptable strategy must include regular feedback collecting, trend analysis, and responsiveness to evolving client preferences.

Customer-centricity enhances brand reputation and goodwill in addition to generating income. Companies that continuously satisfy their customers gain a good reputation and rise in the market. This favorable reputation grows to be a significant advantage, drawing in new clients and strengthening the ties with current ones.

Social media and online reviews have made it easy for customers to share their experiences and shape the opinions of larger audiences. Maintaining a positive online presence becomes contingent upon the comprehension and fulfillment of client demands. Companies that put the needs of their customers first are more likely to get good feedback, recommendations, and testimonials, which improves their online image.

Finally, the demands of the client serve as a compass for ongoing innovation and development. Companies are better positioned to innovate and remain ahead of the competition when they aggressively seek out and implement client input into their procedures. Through the resolution of new issues and demands, these companies maintain their relevance in a changing and dynamic market.

Each business's ability to comprehend and satisfy its customers is essential to its success and survival. It promotes distinction, increases brand loyalty, and enhances favorable brand perception. Businesses that put the needs of their customers first are better able to adapt, develop, and prosper in a cutthroat business climate as markets change and consumer demands rise.

Giving your target audience a tailored experience has become crucial in the fast-paced commercial world of today, when customers are overwhelmed with choices. Businesses are realizing more and more how important it is to build lasting relationships with their clients in addition to providing goods and services. This trend toward customization is more than just a fad; it's a strategic need that promotes customer delight, loyalty, and eventually corporate expansion.

**Recognizing Your Viewership:**

A thorough grasp of your target audience is fundamental to creating individualized experiences. Spend time gathering insights, analyzing consumer behavior, and doing in-depth market research. Understanding the preferences, problems, and goals of your audience paves the way for creating experiences that appeal to them personally.

**Products and Services for Tailoring:**

Equipped with insights, companies may customize their goods and services to match the unique requirements and preferences of their target market. Whether it's combining services, making unique bundles, or altering product features, this degree of care shows a dedication to meeting the needs of each unique consumer.

**Using Information to Make Customizations:**

Data is a treasure trove for developing individualized experiences in the digital era. Use consumer data sensibly and ethically to learn about preferences, engagement trends, and past purchases. Use analytics software and customer relationship management (CRM) systems to further your knowledge and guide customized tactics.

**Tailoring Interaction:**

Building a personal relationship requires communication. Create customized communications that precisely address the issues and passions of your target group. Make use of targeted marketing and segmentation to make sure that your messages speak to particular client categories. Engaging people with personalized emails, newsletters, and social media engagements may be quite effective.

**Crafting Customized User Experiences**

Create individualized customer journeys that account for each client's demands and satisfy them at each touchpoint. Every touchpoint, from the initial conversation to the follow-up, need to be planned with the customer's sense of worth and comprehension in mind. This might entail developing tailored suggestions, interactive material, or special deals predicated on prior actions.

**Using Technology to Make Things More Personal**:

Personalized experiences at scale are made possible by technology, especially machine learning and artificial intelligence (AI). Large-scale statistics may be analyzed by AI algorithms to forecast consumer preferences, automate tailored suggestions, and even offer dynamic pricing depending on user activity.

**Encouraging Customer Selectivity:**

Customization is about giving clients the power to make decisions on their own, not about forcing them to do so. Give consumers the ability to customize their experience, let them add personal touches to their profiles, and give them access to settings that let them decide how personalized their experience is. This methodology honors personal inclinations and cultivates a feeling of control over the client encounter.

## Collecting and Addressing Input:

Continuous improvement is an essential component of customization. Invite clients to share their experiences through feedback, and actively consider their recommendations. To show that you appreciate and consider the opinions of your customers, use feedback loops to improve and fine-tune your customized strategy.

## Harmonizing Automation and Human Input:

Although technology greatly facilitates customization, it is crucial to maintain equilibrium. Bring a human element to all of your encounters, especially when providing customer service. Personalized encounters should exude sincerity and real concern rather than seem artificial.

**Using Metrics to Measure Success:**

Finally, use pertinent metrics to measure the effect of your customized experiences. Examine customer satisfaction ratings, conversion rates, and retention rates. Monitor the success of customized advertising and make ongoing strategy adjustments based on performance information.

Developing tailored experiences is a dynamic and ever-evolving process that necessitates a thorough comprehension of your target audience and a dedication to ongoing enhancement. Through product customization, data analysis, and responsible technology use, companies may create relationships that go beyond sales and encourage advocacy and loyalty. Businesses that put a high priority on providing genuine, customized experiences are well-positioned to not just meet but even surpass customer expectations in the era of customization.

**Customer feedback** is one of the most significant resources in the ever-changing corporate world. Customer feedback is not just an indicator of happiness; it's also an effective instrument for ongoing development. Through proactive consumer feedback collection, analysis, and response, firms may improve their offerings, services, and overall company processes. This iterative strategy promotes long-term success in addition to improving consumer pleasure. Let's examine how companies might use client feedback to drive ongoing development.

1. Create a Feedback Cycle:

Invite clients to share their opinions via social media, reviews, polls, and other platforms. Create a smooth feedback loop so that clients feel appreciated and their thoughts are heard.

2. Actively Listen:Pay attention to what consumers have to say without assuming anything. Positive or negative feedback all provides information about the expectations and experiences of the consumer.

3. Examine Trends and Patterns:

Look past specific remarks to see themes and patterns in the feedback. Recurring themes can draw attention to and identify areas that need work.

4. Set Improvement Priorities:

After patterns are found, rank areas that need improvement according to how they affect customer happiness and corporate goals. Prioritizing issues first guarantees a targeted and successful improvement plan.

5. Transparent Communication:

Inform clients of the modifications you are making in response to their input. Being open and honest fosters trust and shows a dedication to exceeding client expectations.

6. Participation of Employees:

Employees, particularly those that deal directly with customers, should be informed about client feedback. Involve your staff in the process of change, encouraging an organization-wide customer-centric culture.

7. Make Use of Technology:

Make use of technology to expedite the process of gathering and analyzing input. Use analytics tools and customer relationship management (CRM) systems to effectively obtain meaningful information.

8. Ongoing Training: Invest in ongoing training initiatives if employee feedback identifies areas in which they might benefit from more training. Employees that are knowledgeable and well-equipped enhance the client experience.

9. Prospects for Innovation:

Feedback from customers frequently reveals areas for innovation. Examine how ideas for new features, goods, or services that better serve customers might come from recommendations and critiques.

10. Regularly Review and Adjust: As customer expectations change, plans should be reviewed and adjusted as necessary. Maintaining an ongoing feedback loop guarantees that companies remain flexible and adaptable to evolving consumer demands.

11. Express gratitude and acknowledgement:

Thank clients for their input, no matter how favorable or unfavorable. Thanking them affirms the value of their contributions and promotes further participation.

12. Comparison With Rivals:

Compare consumer reviews with rivals' and the industry's benchmarks. Gaining insight into your position within the larger market environment might help you make improvements.

13. Keep an eye on social media:

Monitor consumer sentiment on social media sites. A dedication to client satisfaction may be shown in the public display of good encounters and the resolution of complaints.

14. Putting In Place Initiatives Driven by Feedback:

Create efforts in response to particular comments. Whether it's updating a service procedure or enhancing a function on the internet, feedback-driven projects show a proactive attitude to improvement.

15. Calculate the Effect:

Create key performance indicators (KPIs) to gauge the effects of improvements that have been put into place. Examine data to see how enhancements have affected general business performance and consumer happiness.

**Client feedback** is a dynamic resource that may drive companies toward ongoing development if properly utilized. Organizations may improve their services and establish enduring connections with a pleased and devoted customer base by fostering a culture of listening, responding, and adapting based on consumer feedback.

# Chapter 4

## Agile Entrepreneurship: Adapting to Change

It's now essential to embrace agility in corporate operations to navigate the complexity of today's business environment. Agile companies are better able to innovate, adapt quickly to change, and provide value to their clients. This agility is a mentality and set of behaviors that are transferable to many businesses; it is not industry-specific. This examines the benefits of embracing agility in corporate operations and offers some helpful techniques to do so.

**Switching with the Times:**

Developing a mentality that views change as an opportunity rather than a disruption is essential to embracing agility. Agile companies are flexible and fast to react, swiftly modifying their operations and plans to conform to changing consumer demands, market dynamics, and outside influences.

**Client-First Strategy:**

Agile companies place a high priority on comprehending and satisfying client demands. They may adapt goods and services to changing consumer preferences by regularly obtaining and utilizing client input. This ensures a customer-centric strategy that fosters loyalty and pleasure.

**Interaction Between Cross-Functions:**

Agility might be hampered by silos. Agile companies promote cross-departmental cooperation by removing conventional boundaries. This cooperative strategy encourages a comprehensive understanding of corporate processes, improves problem-solving, and permits the free flow of information.

**Incremental and Iterative Processes:**

By using agile approaches like Scrum or Kanban, projects are divided into more manageable, smaller iterations. Continuous improvement, quick feedback loops, and the ability to change direction in response to new information are all made possible by this iterative method.

**Adaptability in the Distribution of Resources:**

Resource allocation is flexible in agile businesses. Agility helps companies to maximize resources according to short-term demands and long-term goals. This includes modifying workforce numbers, reallocating money, and rearranging priorities.

**Ongoing Education and Development:**
A continual learning culture is fostered by an agile attitude. Teams are able to evaluate their performance, pinpoint areas for development, and iteratively make improvements when they conduct regular feedback loops and retrospectives. This dedication to education promotes creativity and flexibility.

**Technology Enablement:**
Utilize technology to facilitate operations that are more nimble. Business process agility is enhanced by automation, cloud computing, and collaboration technologies. Initiatives aimed at implementing digital transformation can improve communication, expedite processes, and offer decision-makers real-time data.

**Building Strong Teams:**
Agile companies foster autonomy and decentralize decision-making, which empowers

teams. When teams have the power to decide in a way that advances organizational objectives, they are better equipped to react quickly to obstacles. This empowerment encourages accountability and a sense of ownership.

**Quick Testing and Prototyping:**
Agile companies welcome the idea of quick testing and prototyping. Organizations may obtain early input, fine-tune solutions, and prevent protracted development cycles that could result in misaligned products by rapidly generating MVPs, or minimum viable products.

**Adaptable Strategic Planning:**
Although it's still important, agile firms include flexibility into their strategies. Instead of following long-term strategies to the letter, they regularly review and modify their plans in response to changing conditions to make sure they are in line with the reality of the market.

**Leadership Agile:**

Fostering agility requires strong leadership. Agile leaders are open to trying new things, communicative, and have a clear goal. They provide the tone for a flexible and dynamic corporate culture that motivates groups to welcome change and pursue ongoing development.

Adopting agility in company operations is a comprehensive strategy for managing uncertainty and spurring creativity, not only a technique. Agile businesses emphasize adaptation, cooperation, and an unwavering emphasis on delivering value to customers in order to flourish in a fast changing environment. Agility, whether in reaction to changes in the market or internal enhancements, is a driving force behind firms' long-term success.

Agility in company processes requires both flexibility and quick decision-making. In dynamic circumstances, organizations that possess the ability to promptly evaluate events, make well-informed decisions, and adjust to changes are more likely to succeed.

**The following are techniques to improve flexibility and speedy decision-making:**

✓ Decentralized Decision-Making: Give groups and individuals the freedom to decide on their own in their areas of specialization. Decentralization promotes a sense of ownership, expedites decision-making, and lessens bottlenecks.

✓ Data Analytics in Real-Time:
  Use technologies for real-time data analytics to get the most recent information. Organizations can react swiftly to changing market conditions, consumer input, and new trends when decision-making is based on data.

✓ Scenario Planning:
 To foresee possible obstacles and possibilities, prepare scenarios. By using this strategic approach, companies may reduce the amount of time needed to make decisions in the event of unanticipated occurrences by having contingency plans in place.

✓ Practical Approaches:

Use agile approaches like Kanban or Scrum. These frameworks encourage incremental and iterative development, which enables teams to provide value bit by bit and adapt quickly to changing requirements.

✓ Teams with Cross-Funktionality:

Create cross-functional teams by combining people with different backgrounds and viewpoints. These teams are able to work well together, reach choices as a group, and change course fast.

✓ Clearly Stated Frameworks for Decision-Making:

Create explicit organizational decision-making structures. Establish criteria, decision-making authority, and lines of communication to expedite and prevent needless delays in the process.

✓ Emergent Prototyping:

Accept fast prototyping as a means of developing new products or procedures. By using an iterative method, businesses may test and enhance ideas fast, cutting down on time to market and allowing for quick alterations in response to feedback.

✓ Culture of Constant Learning:
Foster an environment where learning and development are ongoing. Teams should be encouraged to take stock of their experiences, draw lessons from both triumphs and setbacks, and use those insights to inform future choices.

✓ Adaptable Resource Distribution:
Retain adaptability while allocating resources. Be ready to quickly reallocate resources in response to opportunities that arise, difficulties that arise, or priorities that change.

✓ Strategic Planning that is Dynamic:
Approach strategic planning with dynamism. Continually review and modify strategic plans in

response to shifts in the marketplace, client demands, and level of competition.

✓ Technology Enablement:
Make use of technology to improve communication, automate repetitive processes, and simplify workflows. Decision-making happens more quickly and with greater operational flexibility when procedures are supported by technology.

✓ Unambiguous Channels of Communication:
   Create effective and transparent avenues of communication. Decision-makers can act more swiftly when pertinent information is communicated to them in a timely and transparent manner.

✓ Policy Flexibility:
   Provide organizational policies that are adaptive and adaptable. Steer clear of unduly inflexible frameworks that might make it difficult to make decisions quickly or adapt to changing conditions.

✓ A Mindset for Innovation:

Encourage the organization to adopt an innovative mentality. Encourage staff members to come up with original ideas, try out new solutions, and be open to taking measured risks.

✓ Pre-established Standards of Judgment:

Establish the criteria for the choice in advance. Making decisions is made easier when there are established standards, particularly in circumstances that happen frequently or routinely.

✓ Timely Evaluations and Modifications:

Set up a schedule for routine evaluations and modifications. Organizations may maintain their agility and responsiveness to changing requirements by regularly evaluating their ongoing initiatives and projects.

Organizations may improve their capacity for swift decision-making and operational flexibility by putting these methods into practice. An agile and resilient corporate environment is produced by empowered teams, data-driven insights, and a continuous improvement culture.

When *facing uncertainty and challenges,* resilience is an essential attribute for both individuals and organizations to possess. It entails having the capacity to adjust, bounce back, and even flourish in the face of difficulty. The following techniques can help cultivate resilience in the face of ambiguities and difficulties:

1. Mentality Modification:

   Develop a growth mentality, which sees obstacles as chances for development. Accept change as a necessary component of the trip and concentrate on the lessons that may be learned from trying circumstances.

2. Adaptive Planning: Create techniques for adaptive planning. Make agile, adaptable plans that can be altered in response to changing conditions rather than strict, long-term plans.

3. Various Viewpoints:

Seek out other viewpoints in your group or company. Diverse perspectives can give creative solutions and a more thorough knowledge of problems.

4. Robust Support Systems:Establish and maintain robust support systems. When things go tough, having a solid support system of friends, family, mentors, and coworkers may offer perspective and emotional support.

5. Continuous Learning: Promote an environment where learning never stops. To put the company in a position to respond to changes and uncertainties, encourage staff members to learn new skills and keep up with industry trends.

6. Sturdy Communication:Continue to communicate in an honest and open manner. Even in uncertain circumstances, keeping stakeholders updated on plans, obstacles, and advancements promotes alignment and trust.

7. Concentrate on Controllables:Direct your attention on elements within your control. Determine which elements of a situation are subject to influence and focus your efforts there.

8. Readiness for Emergencies:

Create strategies for crisis preparation. Plan for possible obstacles, develop reaction plans, and practice often to make sure the company is prepared for unforeseen circumstances.

9. Leadership with Resilience:

Develop tenacious leadership. During times of crisis, leaders who exhibit flexibility, emotional intelligence, and composure set a good example for the entire company.

10. Emotional and Mental Health:

Give your mental and emotional health first priority. Give staff members the tools and assistance they need to deal with stress, worry, and other emotional difficulties that might surface during uncertain times.

11. Divide Difficulties Into Doable Steps:

When faced with big obstacles, divide them into smaller, more doable tasks. This method makes it possible to respond methodically and strategically while preventing feelings of overload.

12. Strategy Flexibility:Be prepared to make strategy adjustments. Organizations are able to

swiftly adjust their plans and tactics in response to changing conditions when they possess flexibility.

13. Celebrate Little Victories:Honor and commemorate your little accomplishments. Acknowledging successes, no matter how small, raises spirits and gives one more reason to overcome obstacles in the future.

14. Promote Team Cohesion:Promote a feeling of unity among the team. Solid team ties foster a caring atmosphere where people are at ease asking for assistance and working together to overcome obstacles.

15. Put an Emphasis on key Values: Base choices and actions on key principles. Maintaining a feeling of purpose and serving as a compass in unpredictable times are two benefits of aligning with company principles.

16. Consider and Acquire:

   After overcoming obstacles, give yourself some time to think and grow. Analyze what went well, what may be done better, and use the knowledge gained to strengthen resilience in similar circumstances in the future.

17. Promote Innovation:Promote innovation as a way to overcome obstacles. Creative ideas that might aid in efficiently navigating uncertainty are frequently the result of innovative thinking.

18. Keep a Long-Term view:Keep a long-term view in mind while dealing with current issues. Recognize that there will inevitably be unknowns along the way, and that resilience calls for perseverance over an extended period of time.

Through the application of these tactics, people and organizations may establish resilience as a fundamental strength that will empower them to successfully traverse unpredictable and challenging situations with increased adaptability, tenacity, and success.

# Chapter 5

## Sustainable Practices: Balancing Profit and Purpose

Not only is it morally required, but incorporating sustainability into corporate operations may also be a calculated strategic move that will pay off in the long run. Businesses may secure their own resilience and competitiveness while making beneficial contributions to society by balancing environmental, social, and economic issues. The following are some methods for successfully incorporating sustainability into corporate operations:

1. Clearly State Your Sustainability Objectives:
   Establish time-bound, quantifiable, and precise sustainability targets that are in line with the mission and values of your company. These

objectives may include social responsibility, environmental preservation, and economic sustainability.

2. Carry Out Audits for Sustainability:
   Use sustainability audits to evaluate your present company procedures. Determine where waste reduction, resource efficiency, and social effect may all be improved.

3. Management of Sustainable Supply Chains:
   Collaborate with vendors who are as dedicated to sustainability as you are. Adopt sustainable sourcing techniques to guarantee that all supply chain participants follow moral and ecologically sound guidelines.

4. Conservation and Energy Efficiency:
   Make investments in energy-saving devices and methods. To lessen your impact on the environment, cut back on energy use, look into renewable energy sources, and put conservation measures in place.

## 5. Recycling and Waste Reduction:

Adopt waste minimization techniques and encourage recycling in your company. Examine methods to reduce the amount of trash produced and look at possibilities to recycle or repurpose items.

## 6. Social Responsibility Programs:

Create and promote social responsibility initiatives that enhance community well-being. This might involve collaborations with nearby groups, humanitarian endeavors, or community development activities.

## 7. Involving Stakeholders:

Interact with stakeholders to learn about their expectations for sustainability, such as staff members, clients, investors, and the neighborhood. Take their suggestions into account for your sustainability projects, and be open and honest about your development.

## 8.Practices of the Circular Economy:

Adopt the tenets of the circular economy by creating long-lasting, repairable, and recyclable products. Look for ways to recycle or repurpose materials in your manufacturing operations.

9. Employee Engagement and Training:Promote an environmentally conscious culture among staff members and teach them about sustainable practices. Employee engagement may play a significant role in supporting sustainability initiatives both inside and beyond the company.

10. Green Building methods: Adopt green building methods, where appropriate. Buildings should be designed, built, or renovated with an emphasis on eco-friendly materials, water conservation, and energy efficiency.

11. Carbon impact Reduction:Create plans to lessen the carbon impact of your company. This might entail using low-carbon transportation choices, investing in carbon-neutral technology, or offsetting emissions.

12. Sustainable Product Development: Make sure to include sustainability in the process of developing new products. Take into account how raw materials, production methods, and the product's life cycle will affect the environment.

13. Disclosure and Openness:
   Disseminate sustainability reports that outline the achievements and performance of your company. Transparency shows a commitment to taking responsibility for your sustainability initiatives and fosters confidence among stakeholders.

14. Adherence to Regulations:
   Remain aware of and abide by all applicable environmental laws. Deal with compliance concerns proactively and make every effort to go above and beyond regulatory standards.

15. Ongoing Enhancement:
   Consider sustainability as an ongoing process of progress. Review and adapt your sustainability programs on a regular basis in

response to changing stakeholder expectations, emerging best practices, and technology developments.

16. Standards and Certification:
   Acquire certifications from reputable sustainability groups and follow guidelines. A third-party's endorsement of your dedication to sustainable business practices can be obtained through certifications.

17. Cooperation and Joint Ventures:
   Work together with colleagues in the industry, non-governmental organizations, and governmental agencies to exchange best practices and tackle shared sustainability issues. Collaborations have the power to increase the effect of sustainability programs.

By *using these tactics, companies may improve their reputation, draw* in environmentally concerned clients and investors, and have a good social effect in addition to helping to create a more sustainable world. Achieving sustainability is a journey that calls for dedication, creativity, and a comprehensive strategy for striking a balance between financial gain and social and environmental accountability.

Creating a brand that is socially conscious requires incorporating environmental responsibility, social impact, and ethical principles into many facets of your company's operations. This is a comprehensive strategy for building a brand that is socially conscious:

Explain Your Purpose and Values:
   Give a purpose and set of clear ideals that are in line with social responsibility. Making decisions will be based on this foundation, which will appeal to customers who value ethical companies.

Product Chain and Ethical Sourcing:
   Make sure that your supply chain procedures follow moral guidelines. In your procurement of raw materials and production procedures, place a

strong emphasis on human rights, fair labor practices, and environmental sustainability.

Community Support and Engagement: Assist and interact with your local community. Form alliances, make contributions to community development initiatives, and get staff members involved in volunteer work to show your dedication to social responsibility.

Well-being of Employees:
   Give your employees' well-being first priority. Assure equitable compensation, secure working environments, and chances for career advancement. Create an environment at work that values diversity and inclusiveness.

Openness and Responsibility:
   Accept openness in all aspects of your business. Talk honestly about your sources, effects, and business methods. Accept responsibility for your errors and show that you're dedicated to making improvements over time.

Creative and Sustainable Practices:
   Include eco-friendly procedures in your business operations. Use waste-reduction strategies, energy-efficient practices, and sustainable options while designing and producing products.

Responsibility for the Product:
   Provide goods that are long-lasting, recyclable, and have as little of an impact on the environment as possible. Give customers all the knowledge they need to make educated decisions by clearly communicating product details, such as sourcing and disposal policies.

Social Impact Initiatives:
Start social impact projects and take an active part in them. Whether it's promoting healthcare, education, or environmental preservation, match your brand to issues that are important to both your target market and your principles.

All-inclusive Promotion & Marketing:

Make sure the campaigns you run for marketing and advertising are courteous and inclusive. Represent a range of viewpoints, steer clear of prejudices, and support constructive social narratives.

Just Prices and Availability:
Aim for reasonable costs and ease of access. Strike a balance between affordability and profitability to expand the market for your goods and services and promote social inclusion.

Education for Consumers:
Inform them about your socially conscious business operations. Make it clear to them how their decisions have an influence and highlight how their support leads to favorable social and environmental consequences.

Work together with stakeholders:
To increase the effect of your socially conscious activities, work together with stakeholders like NGOs, colleagues in the business, and governmental organizations.

Systemic problems can be more successfully addressed by group initiatives.

Assess and Document Effect:
   Put benchmarks in place to assess the results of your socially conscious endeavors. Report on your development on a regular basis to show that you are dedicated to responsibility and ongoing development.

Flexibility and Ongoing Development:
   Remain flexible and dedicated to ongoing development. Accept criticism, keep up with new developments in best practices, and modify your plans to optimize your beneficial social and environmental impacts.

Maintaining a constant dedication to moral behavior, openness, and constructive social influence is necessary to develop a socially conscious brand. By incorporating these ideas into your company plan, you can build a brand that appeals to ethical customers while simultaneously making a positive impact on the planet.

Businesses are realizing more and more how important sustainable efforts are to their long-term survival in an era where social responsibility and environmental awareness are on the rise. Sustainability has developed into a strategic imperative that helps society and the environment as well as greatly enhancing an organization's resilience and competitiveness. It is no longer just about following rules or being philanthropic.

Sustainable initiatives cover a wide range of activities, including ethical sourcing, community involvement, ecologically sensitive operations, and employee well-being. These projects' interconnectedness has a knock-on impact that goes beyond direct environmental concerns to affect consumer views, staff involvement, and the company's reputation as a whole.

Growing brand loyalty and drawing in eco-aware customers are two of the main ways that sustainable efforts support long-term success. Today's shoppers are becoming more conscious of the moral and environmental consequences of the things they buy. Companies that exhibit a dedication to sustainability not only satisfy this discriminating clientele but also gain their confidence and allegiance. A company's reputation for moral behavior turns into a valuable asset that feeds into a positive feedback loop where happy consumers recommend the brand to others, which promotes steady growth.

Furthermore, operational improvements and cost reductions are frequently the result of sustainable efforts. Energy-saving techniques, trash minimization, and sustainable sourcing are examples of practices that benefit the bottom line in addition to being environmentally responsible. Businesses that make investments in environmentally friendly technology and procedures frequently find that these projects pay off financially over time, making them appear more flexible and robust in the face of resource limitations and economic ups and downs.

Sustainable initiatives are essential for drawing and keeping top talent in the field of employee engagement. Working with companies that share their values is highly valued by today's workforce. Positive work cultures are produced by organizations that put an emphasis on the well-being of their employees, provide sustainable practices, and take part in social responsibility programs. Consequently, this boosts worker contentment, output, and allegiance, adding to the organization's sustained prosperity and stability.

Partnerships and collaborations are impacted positively by sustainable activities, which have an effect even outside of the immediate organizational limits. Companies that put sustainability first are more likely to draw in collaborators, investors, and suppliers that share their values. Business connections are improved when values and a dedication to moral behavior are in harmony. This creates chances for strategic alliances and common objectives that support sustained success.

Furthermore, businesses that actively adopt sustainable practices are better positioned to handle regulatory changes as regulatory frameworks throughout the world shift to address environmental and social issues. In addition to reducing regulatory risks, being ahead of compliance obligations presents the company to regulators, clients, and investors as a responsible and progressive corporation.

There are many different and significant ways that sustainable projects affect long-term performance. Beyond the observable advantages of financial savings and improved operational effectiveness, sustainability increases overall organizational resilience, draws in top talent, and builds brand loyalty. Businesses that embrace sustainable initiatives are not only making a positive impact on the world but also securing their position as leaders in an era where sustainability will be a critical success factor. This is because businesses are becoming more aware of the interconnectedness of economic, social, and environmental factors.

# Innovate to Elevate Worksheet

| Self-Reflection | **Define Your Entrepreneurial Goals**<br>☐ List your short-term and long-term business goals.<br>☐ Prioritize them based on their importance to your overall |
|---|---|

| | |
|---|---|
| | vision.<br>**Assess Your Current Business Position**<br>☐ Identify your strengths, weaknesses, opportunities, and threats (SWOT analysis).<br>☐ Reflect on your current market position and customer feedback. |
| Key Concepts from the Book | **Core Concepts**<br>☐ Summarize the key concepts presented in "Innovate to Elevate."<br>**Application to Your Business**<br>☐ How can these concepts be |

| | |
|---|---|
| | applied to your specific business?<br>☐ Identify areas where innovation can be incorporated. |
| Action Plan | **Prioritize Innovative Strategies**<br>☐ Choose specific strategies from the book that align with your business goals.<br>**Implementation Steps**<br>☐ Break down each chosen strategy into actionable steps.<br>☐ Define responsible parties and timelines for implementation. |

| Measure Progress | **Key Performance Indicators (KPIs)**<br>☐ Identify measurable KPIs to track the success of your innovative strategies.<br>☐ Set realistic benchmarks for each KPI.<br>**Regular Evaluation**<br>☐ Schedule regular reviews to assess the effectiveness of implemented strategies.<br>☐ Adjust your plan based on feedback and evolving business conditions. |
|---|---|
| Reflection and | **Lessons Learned** |

| Learning | ☐ Document lessons learned from the implementation process. ☐ Identify what worked well and areas for improvement. **Continuous Learning** ☐ Outline a plan for ongoing learning and staying updated on innovative business practices. |
|---|---|

www.ingramcontent.com/pod-product-compliance
Lightning Source LLC
Chambersburg PA
CBHW071213290526
45796CB00008B/229